STAN AND ALLEN

A BOOK ABOUT GENDER

WORDS + PICTURES BY HUXLEY REN BUNN

Archway Publishing books may be ordered through booksellers or by contacting:

Archway Publishing
1663 Liberty Drive
Bloomington, IN 47403
www.archwaypublishing.com
844-669-3957

ISBN: 978-1-6657-3117-1 (sc)
ISBN: 978-1-6657-3118-8 (hc)
ISBN: 978-1-6657-3116-4 (e)

Print information available on the last page.

Archway Publishing rev. date: 10/21/2022

MY GOODNESS WHAT A SUNNY DAY

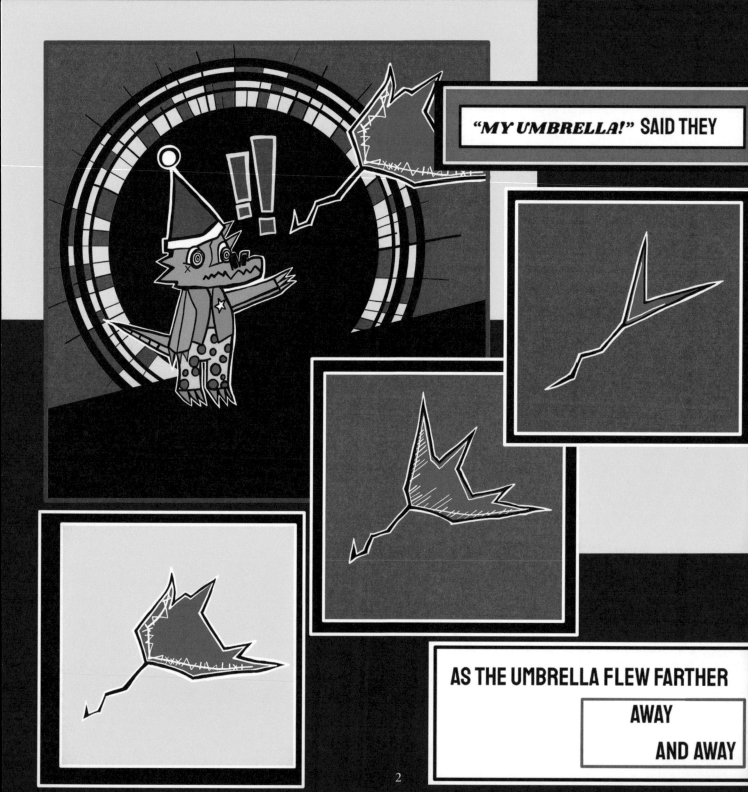

ALLEN PAUSED,
"STAN,
YOU'RE AN ALLIGATOR
IN SUMMER.
WHY DO YOU NEED
AN UMBRELLA,
ISN'T IT A BUMMER?"

*"WITHOUT IT
I'M ALWAYS
SUNBURNT
AND HURT!"*

"IT'S TRUE,
YOU SHOULD ALWAYS DO
WHAT'S BEST FOR YOU."
ALLEN AGREES.

"WANT TO GO GET
SOME LEMONADE?"
ALLEN ASKED.
"WE HAVEN'T BEEN TO THE
MUD SLUG IN A DECADE!"

STAN SMILED
AND SHOUTED, *"SURE THING*

CHICKEN WING!"

"**ONE COFFEE AND ONE LEMONADE PLEASE!**"

STAN ORDERS

GREGORY ANSWERS, "SURE GENTLEMAN, THAT'S A BREEZE."

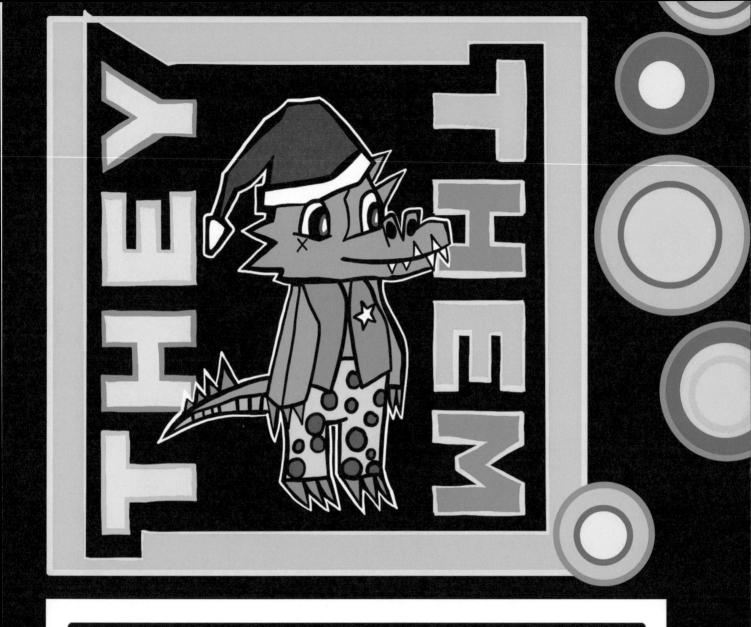

ALLEN PAUSES, "ACTUALLY THEY PREFER GENDER NEUTRAL PRONOUNS."

"I'M SO SORRY,
DIDN'T MEAN TO GET YOU DOWN.
WHAT SHOULD I SAY INSTEAD?"
GREGORY SAID WITH A FROWN.

ALWAYS ASK

WITH A WARM SMILE STAN JUMPS IN,

"YOU CAN ALWAYS GO WITH

GENDER NEUTRAL GREETINGS

LIKE SURE YOU TWO, HERE YOU GO FOLKS, HERE FRIENDS,

OR

ALWAYS ASK!

IT SEEMS LIKE A LOT OF EXTRA EFFORT FOR AN EXTRA TASK

BUT TRUST ME

IT COULD MAKE

ALL THE DIFFERENCE IN A HUGE WAY

IN SOMEONE'S DAY!"

GREGORY STOPS TO ASK, "HOW COULD IT HURT SOMEONE TO BE REFERRED TO THAT WAY?"

"HOW WOULD IT MAKE YOU FEEL TO HAVE SOMEONE REFER TO YOU AS

YOU AS

MS.,

MA'AM, OR

HER

ALL THE TIME?" STAN EXPLAINS

"NOT GOOD!" SAID GREGORY WITH A QUICK CHIME. "I REALLY LIKE BEING A BOY! SO WHAT EXACTLY SHOULD I ASK NOW THAT I HAVE THIS INFO TO ENJOY?"

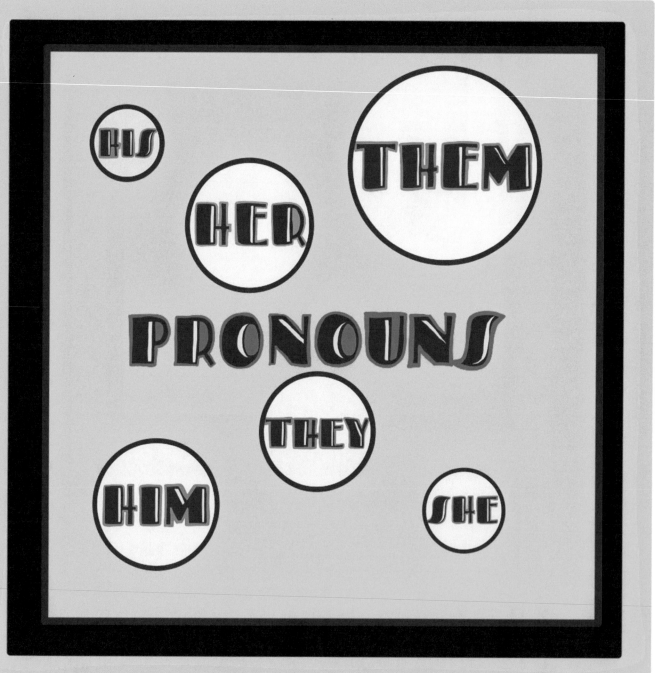

"ASK SOMEONE WHAT PRONOUNS THEY USE." STAN ANSWERS, "I IDENTIFY AS NON-BINARY AND USE THEY / THEM PRONOUNS. THEY / THEM IS WHAT I CHOOSE."

PRONOUN
A WORD THAT TAKES THE PLACE OF A NOUN.

GREGORY ASKS WITH CONFUSION, "NON-BINARY?"

"YUP! I'M NON-BINARY."

STAN DESCRIBES.

"IT'S ABOUT GENDER.

IT MEANS I DON'T

IDENTIFY AS A GIRL OR AS A BOY."

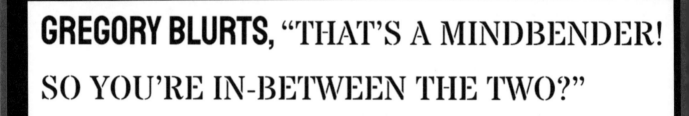

GREGORY BLURTS, "THAT'S A MINDBENDER! SO YOU'RE IN-BETWEEN THE TWO?"

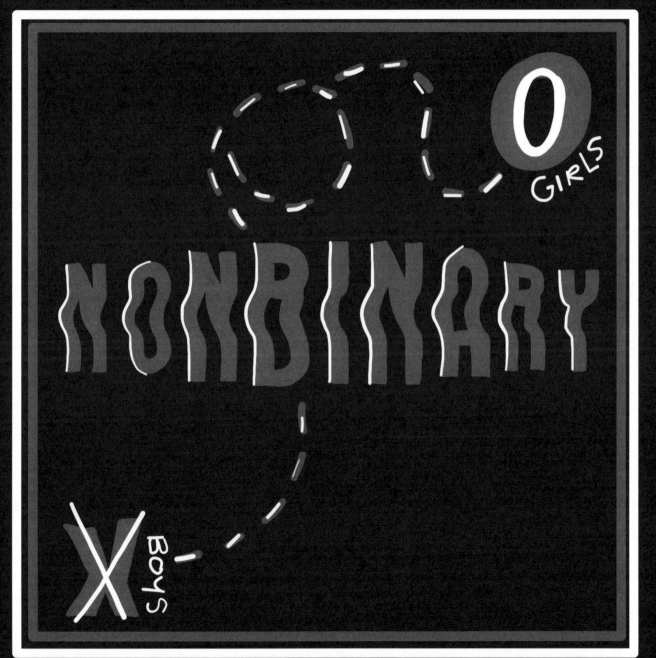

STAN ILLUSTRATES,

"NOT EXACTLY, LET'S TALK THIS THROUGH. THINK OF GENDER LIKE A COLOR WHEEL. IF BOYS ARE BLUE AND GIRLS ARE RED YOU MIGHT THINK THAT EVERYONE ELSE IS PURPLE — BUT IN REALITY THERE IS A WHOLE COLOR WHEEL OF IDENTITY OUT THERE! AS LONG AS YOU FEEL COMFORTABLE WITH YOUR GENDER THEN WHATEVER YOU CHOSE IS PERFECT!"

GREGORY SMILES BIG AND SAYS, "I LIKE THAT, I'M HAPPY TO BE DIRECT."

RYAN ENTERS THE MUD SLUG ASKING,

"ANYONE SEEN A GIRL
WHO LOST HER UMBRELLA?"

"*ACTUALLY THAT'S MY UMBRELLA!*"
STAN CALLS OUT.

RYAN STOPS, "*BUT IT'S PINK?*"

STAN EXCLAIMS WITH JOY,
"*ANYONE CAN LIKE PINK!*"

RYAN STOMPS, *"PINK IS FOR GIRLS!"*

STAN CLARIFYS, *"I'M NON-BINARY AND I LOVE PINK. ESPECIALLY PINK PEARLS!"*

"SO YOU LIKE GIRLS AND BOYS?" RYAN QUESTIONS

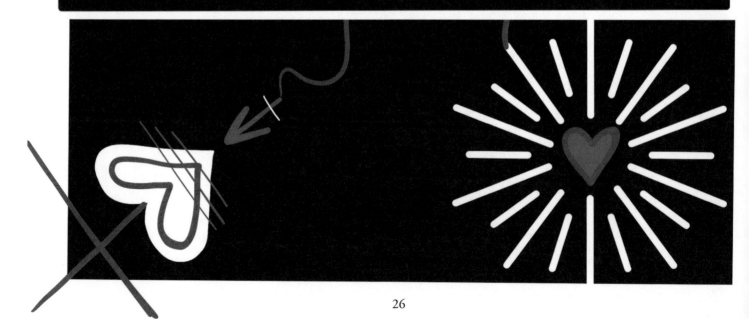

STAN REPLYS,

"NOPE—

YOUR GENDER HAS NOTHING TO DO

WITH YOUR ROMANTIC FEELINGS. BEING NON-BINARY

DOESN'T DETERMINE WHO YOU LIKE OR LOVE DEAR

AND TENDER.

IT'S ALL ABOUT YOUR OWN INNER FEELING OF GENDER.

NON-BINARY IS JUST A GENDER LABEL —

LIKE BOY OR GIRL."

RYAN REACTS WITH A SMILE,

" OKAY, THANKS FOR EXPLAINING.

LET ME GIVE IT A WHIRL.

HERE'S YOUR UMBRELLA FRIEND."

WITH THE BIGGEST SMILE STAN SAYS, " *THANKS FRIEND!*

I THOUGHT MY UMBRELLA WAS AT ITS END."

NON-BINARY DEFINITION :

SOMEONE WHO DOES NOT
IDENTIFY AS EXCLUSIVELY A MAN
OR WOMAN.
(IDENTIFYING OUTSIDE THE BINARY GENDERS)
SOMEONE WHO IS NON-BINARY
MIGHT FEEL LIKE
A MIX OF GENDERS OR
LIKE THEY HAVE NO GENDER AT ALL.
IT'S DIFFERENT FOR EVERYONE.

KEY THINGS TO REMEMBER!

1. NOT EVERYONE WHO IS NON-BINARY USES THEY / THEM PRONOUNS, JUST ASK!

2. GENDER HAS NOTHING TO DO WITH SEXUAL ORIENTATION. JUST LIKE BEING A BOY DOESN'T DETERMINE IF YOU LIKE BOYS OR GIRLS BEING NON-BINARY DOESN'T DETERMINE WHO YOU ROMANTICALLY LIKE.

3. IT'S OKAY TO HAVE QUESTIONS AND ASK THEM!

SOME FUN GENDER NEUTRAL GREETINGS TO TRY:

1. HOW'S IT GOING FRIENDS?
2. HOW IS EVERYONE?
3. HOW ARE YOU FOLKS?
4. HELLO THERE!
5. HI CREW!
6. GOOD MORNING EVERYONE.
7. GOODNIGHT Y'ALL.
8. CHEERS FRIENDS!

ABOUT HUXLEY REN BUNN

Huxley Ren Bunn identifies as non-binary and uses he/him, they/them pronouns. His writing is inspired by his own difficult experiences coming out to people who are unsure about what being non-binary means. Huxley is excited to help educate others with his first children's book.

Printed in the United States
by Baker & Taylor Publisher Services